Trent's Deep Sea Discovery

Exploring Underwater Life

Written by Barrington Scott
Illustrated by Ananta Mohanta

Trent's Adventures Deep Sea Discovery

Copyright @ Barrington Scott

Published by Adventure Atlas Publishing

What's Scuba Diving?

Scuba diving is an exciting underwater activity that involves using special gear, including a breathing through an oxygen tank to explore the world beneath the ocean's surface. As a scuba diver, you'll feel weightless underwater, get up close to sea animals, and marvel at the stunning sights of coral reefs and other underwater landscapes. It's like entering a magical world, giving you the chance to discover and enjoy the ecosystems .

Guess what? You can kick off your scuba diving adventure if you're 10 years or older. Just ask your parent or guardian to check out diving programs that will let you begin your underwater course!

Your Scuba Gear Essentials

Fins

Special flipper-like shoes that scuba divers wear on their feet to help them swim faster and move more easily underwater.

Oxygen Tank

A metal tank that allows them to breathe underwater while having an exciting time and, staying safe!

Snorkel Full Face Mask

A snorkel mask helps a diver see underwater by covering their eyes and nose. This way they can explore the underwater world and enjoy the beauty beneath the surface

BCD "Buoyancy Control Device"

A vest that helps scuba divers float or sink in the water so they can move up, down, or stay in one place

Coral is like a house for many sea creatures - almost 25% of all ocean creatures live there! But that's not all coral does. Coral also helps keep the water clean by acting like a big strainer that collects trash and filters the water. That means lots of tiny living things like bacteria, plants, and animals work together to make sure the ocean stays healthy and clean!

Fun facts about corals:

Did you know that corals are actually living animals? Even though there are more than a thousand types of coral, they can be split into six groups because they are made up of very small creatures called polyps.

- Small polyp stony
- Large polyp stony
- Zoanthids
- Soft
- Gorgonians
- Mushrooms

Wow! Take a look at this coral! It's quite vibrant and colorful

Fun facts about salmon:

- Did you know that salmon can live in both fresh and salty water?
- Salmon have an amazing sense of smell that helps them find their way back to their birthplace, even after years in the ocean.
- These fish are super strong and can jump up to 6 feet high to get over obstacles in their way!
- Salmon are really important to the environment because they help bring nutrients to other animals and plants.

Trent: Look at all the different kinds of fish. Let's check to see whats here.

Fun facts about angel fish:

- Did you know that as an angelfish gets older, its colors can change? For example, black stripes might turn into yellow ones! Their colors can also be affected by things like health, nutrition, and breeding.

- Angelfish have a thin, pancake-like body shape that helps them fit through tight spaces and cracks in coral reefs. This helps them stay safe from predators and find food.

- There are 90 different types of angelfish in the world.

Fun facts about pufferfish:

• The most lethal fish in the ocean is the puffer.

• Did you know that puffer fish are the only fish without eyelids that can still close their eyes? They pull their eyeballs back and close the skin around their eyes.

• Puffer fish can puff up to three to four times their size when they're scared. They do this by swallowing lots of water really quickly, which makes them look like a spiny ball.

• There are more than 200 different types of puffer fish that live in both fresh and salt water. They come in all sorts of shapes, sizes, and colors!

Fun facts about lionfish:

• Did you know that lionfish have 18 pointed spines on their back, belly, and rear fins? These spines are covered in sheaths and have venom glands at their bases.

• Female lionfish can lay up to 2 million eggs in one year! That's a lot of baby lionfish! They can even lay up to 30,000 eggs in less than a week.

• Lionfish can eat up to 30 times their own stomach volume! That's like eating 30 full meals in one sitting!

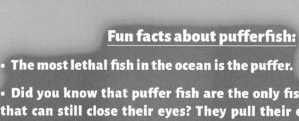

Pufferfish

Lionfish

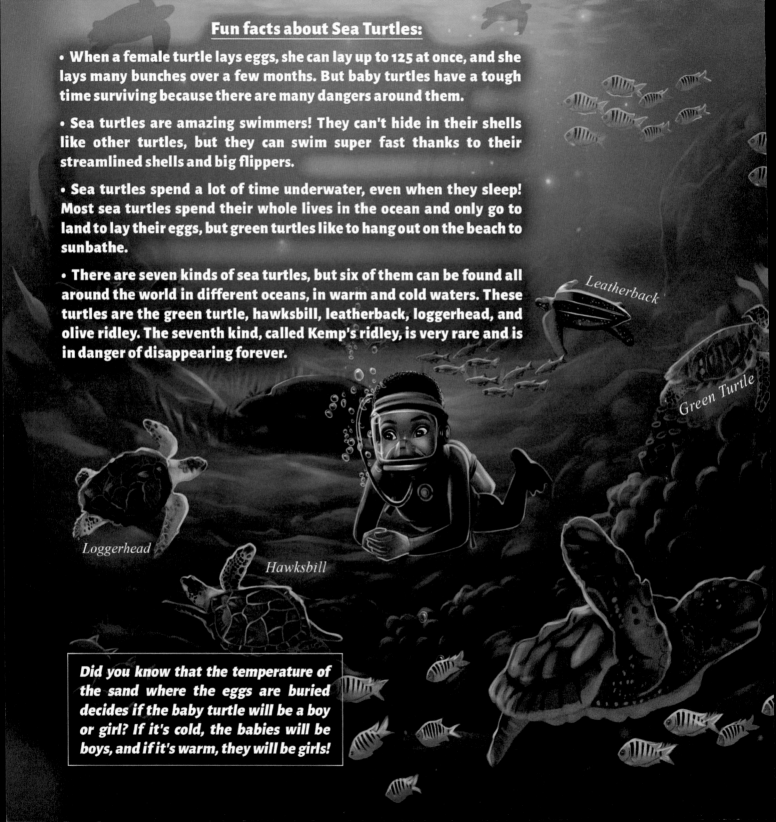

Fun facts about Sea Turtles:

• When a female turtle lays eggs, she can lay up to 125 at once, and she lays many bunches over a few months. But baby turtles have a tough time surviving because there are many dangers around them.

• Sea turtles are amazing swimmers! They can't hide in their shells like other turtles, but they can swim super fast thanks to their streamlined shells and big flippers.

• Sea turtles spend a lot of time underwater, even when they sleep! Most sea turtles spend their whole lives in the ocean and only go to land to lay their eggs, but green turtles like to hang out on the beach to sunbathe.

• There are seven kinds of sea turtles, but six of them can be found all around the world in different oceans, in warm and cold waters. These turtles are the green turtle, hawksbill, leatherback, loggerhead, and olive ridley. The seventh kind, called Kemp's ridley, is very rare and is in danger of disappearing forever.

Leatherback

Green Turtle

Loggerhead

Hawksbill

Did you know that the temperature of the sand where the eggs are buried decides if the baby turtle will be a boy or girl? If it's cold, the babies will be boys, and if it's warm, they will be girls!

Chrysaora
(jellysfish species)

Lions mane

Pelagia

Aurelia

Cotylorhiza

Fun facts about jellyfish:

• Jellyfish are really old! Scientists think they might be over 700 million years old, but it's hard to find their fossils because they don't have bones.

• Jellyfish don't have a brain, and most of their body is made of water (98% to be exact!)

• There are over 2,000 different kinds of jellyfish all around the world.

• When a special kind of jellyfish called Turritopsis dohrnii gets scared or sick or old, it can turn back into a baby jellyfish! It transforms its cells into a younger version of itself, like magic!

Did you know that jellyfish are 98% water?

Fun facts about Squids:

• Giant squids are some of the biggest creatures in the ocean! They can grow to be as long as a school bus and weigh more than 600 pounds!

• Squids are super speedy swimmers and can swim as fast as a car on the highway!

• Squids are smart and have a special way of getting away from danger called "jet pro-pul-sion," where they squirt water to escape from predators.

Squids and octopuses are both called "ce-pha-lo-pods". They look similar in some ways, but they also have important differences. They live in different places, have different body shapes, and behave differently.

Smoothskin

Dumbo

Bluering

Seven Arm

Fun facts about octopuses:

- Octopuses are really old! The oldest octopus fossil ever found is about 296 million years old!

- Did you know that octopuses have three hearts? Two of them help the octopus breathe, while the other one helps the organs.

- An octopus's arms are super smart! In fact, they have two-thirds of the octopus's brain power. That's why they can do things like open a mussel for food while the rest of the body is busy exploring.

- There are over 300 kinds of octopuses in every ocean around the world!

North Pacific Giant

Atlantic Pygmy

Mimic

Fun facts about seahorses:

• Seahorses are special because they find a partner and stay with them forever. This means they only mate with one other seahorse!

• Seahorses have really cool eyes that work independently of each other. This lets them keep an eye out for danger in all directions at the same time.

• Seahorses have a unique way of swimming, they use their dorsal fin to propel themselves forward, and their pectoral fins to steer and hover.

• The male seahorse carries the eggs in a pouch on his belly and is responsible for caring for the developing embryos until they hatch.

Fun facts about sea urchins:

• Sea urchins come in 950 different species.

• There are no bones in them.

• A sea urchin water-moving spines allow it to bounce about the seafloor.

• Sea urchins are able to regrow lost spines, and in some cases, even entire limbs.

Fun facts about sea snakes:

• There are 69 types of sea snakes!

• Sea snakes are special because they can have babies underwater.

• Sea snakes can absorb some of the air they need through their skin, which means they can stay underwater for a long time, up to 8 hours!

• Even though they live in water, sea snakes can still get thirsty, so they sometimes swim to the land to find fresh water.

• Watch out for some sea snakes! Their venom is even stronger than a cobra's!

Sea Snake

Moray Eel

Conger Eel

Fun facts about eels:

• More than 400 different species of eels exist.

• Eels can live in both fresh and salt water.

• Eels can navigate about reefs without getting scratched because of their mucus-covered bodies.

Orca

Question: Why are killer whales called so if they are actually dolphins? Ancient mariners who saw orcas hunting and consuming other whale species gave them the name "killer whale."

Did you know? Dolphins are super fast swimmers! They can zip through the water going fast as 37 miles per hour.

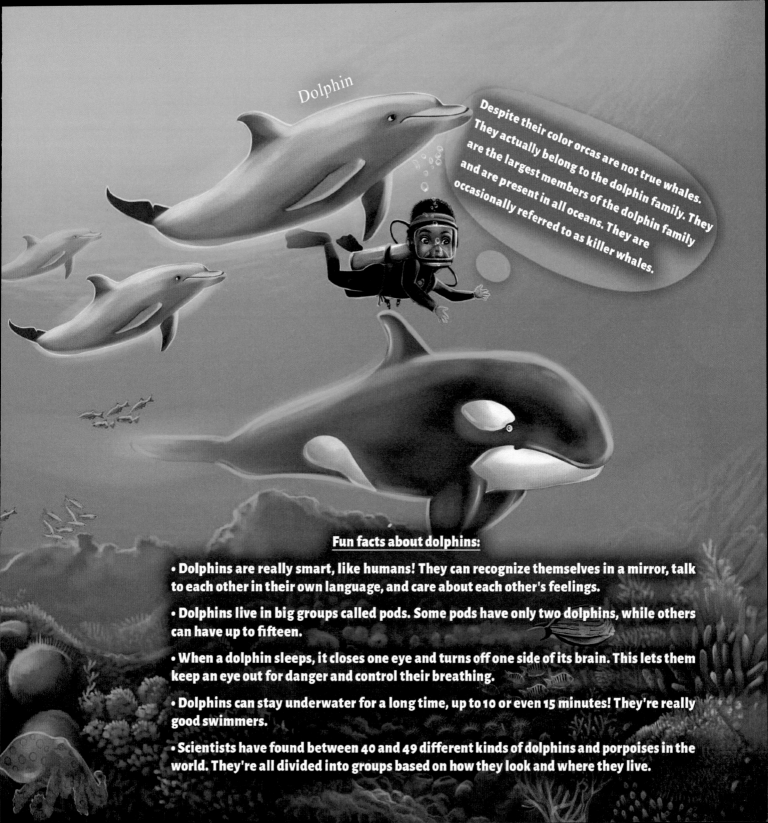

Dolphin

Despite their color orcas are not true whales. They actually belong to the dolphin family. They are the largest members of the dolphin family and are present in all oceans. They are occasionally referred to as killer whales.

Fun facts about dolphins:

• Dolphins are really smart, like humans! They can recognize themselves in a mirror, talk to each other in their own language, and care about each other's feelings.

• Dolphins live in big groups called pods. Some pods have only two dolphins, while others can have up to fifteen.

• When a dolphin sleeps, it closes one eye and turns off one side of its brain. This lets them keep an eye out for danger and control their breathing.

• Dolphins can stay underwater for a long time, up to 10 or even 15 minutes! They're really good swimmers.

• Scientists have found between 40 and 49 different kinds of dolphins and porpoises in the world. They're all divided into groups based on how they look and where they live.

Manta Ray

Did you know?

Stingrays and manta rays are not the same despite frequently being grouped together. The mouth of a stingray is positioned on its underside, whereas that of a manta ray is found along the front edge of its body. Manta rays dwell in the open ocean rather than on the seafloor and lack the stingray's distinctive tail barb or stinger.

Fun facts about manta rays:

• Manta rays have spots on their bellies that are unique to each individual, similar to how people have different fingerprints.

• Manta rays have big brains compared to other fish.

• Manta rays can sometimes jump out of the water, just like how pizzas can sometimes fly out of ovens!

Fun facts about sting rays:

• There are over 600 different kinds of skates and rays in the world.

• Stingrays are related to sharks and their bodies are made of cartilage instead of bones like humans have.

• Although their venom is not usually deadly to people, stingrays can cause a lot of pain, swelling, and other uncomfortable symptoms.

• Stingrays can hide really well by blending into their environment, which helps them stay safe from predators.

• Stingrays have been around for a really long time - even when the dinosaurs were still alive!

Stingray

Skate

Did you know that skates are flat bodied cartilaginous fish? The quickest way to tell them apart is by looking at their tails. Stingrays have long whip like tails; skates tails tend to be thick and short

Blue Whale

Finback whale

Fun facts about humpback whales

- Did you know that humpback whales have a big hump on their back? That's where they get their name!

- Humpback whales are really big, about the size of two school buses put together! They can be up to 50 feet long and weigh as much as 8 elephants!

- Every year, humpback whales go on really long trips. They can swim up to 5000 miles! That's like swimming across the whole United States two times!

Humpback whales can live a really long time, up to 90 years! That's older than most people's grandparents!

Fun facts about blue whales:

• Did you know that blue whales are the biggest animals ever to exist? They can be as long as 100 feet (30 meters) and weigh as much as 50 elephants!

• Even though they are so huge, blue whales eat tiny animals called krill, which they filter out of the water using their special mouth parts.

• Blue whales are really loud! Their voices can be as loud as a jet engine and can travel over 500 miles (800 kilometers) under the water!

Minke Whale

Sperm Whale

Right Whale

Fun facts about sperm whales:

• Sperm whales have the biggest brains in the world, even larger than humans!

• They can dive really deep, up to 3,000 feet, to catch squids and other prey. And they can hold their breath for up to 90 minutes!

• Sperm whale males can weigh up to 87,000 pounds, which is as heavy as about 12 elephants. Females are a bit smaller, weighing up to 27,000 pounds.

• Female sperm whales give birth to a calf every 5 to 7 years, after carrying the baby for 14 to 16 months.

Sand Ti_

Blacktip

Tigershark

Thresher

Fun facts about sharks:

• Sharks are a special kind of fish with no bones in their body, only cartilage!

• Sharks have special organs on their nose, eyes, and mouth that let them sense changes in ocean temperature and electromagnetic fields.

• Shark skin is rough because it has tiny teeth on it, called dermal denticles, which help sharks swim faster.

• Sharks have been around for a really long time, around 500 million years.

• Hammerhead sharks have eyes on the sides of their flat heads, which let them see in every direction at once. This helps them hunt and avoid other animals.

Hammerhead

Whale Shark

Fun facts about whale sharks:

• Whale sharks are not whales, but actually a kind of shark with unique markings on their skin.

• Each whale shark's markings are like a fingerprint and can be used to tell them apart.

• Whale sharks can live for about 70 years.

• Whale sharks are the biggest sharks to currently exist outside of the megalodons, which disappeared about 2.5 million years ago.

• There are more than 500 different kinds of sharks. • Sharks have to keep swimming in order to breathe, so they never take a nap or rest like we do.

Fun facts about the ocean:

• Did you know that the ocean is in danger because of pollution? That's right! Every year, about 8 million tons of garbage end up in the ocean, which is as heavy as 59,000 blue whales! Wow!

• Also, did you know that plastic takes a looong time to break down? It can take anywhere from 400 to 1000 years! That's a really long time!

• There's also a really big garbage dump in the Great Pacific Ocean that's twice the size of Texas! Can you imagine that?

More facts about the ocean:

- 70% of the surface of the world is covered by the water and is home to about 94 percent of the world's animal species.

- The oceans produce more than 70% of the oxygen that exists on Earth.

- The ocean contains over 20 million tons of gold.

- The ocean is blue because of the sun.

- Oceanic volcanism accounts for 90% of all volcanic activity on Earth.

- On the ocean floor, there are thought to be more than 3 million shipwrecks.

- Unfortunately, pollution can hurt a lot of animals in the ocean, like sea turtles, whales, and seabirds. When they eat plastic, it can make them very sick. That's why we need to be careful with our trash!

- Overfishing and bad fishing practices can also hurt the ocean. When we take too many fish out of the water or use big nets that scrape the ocean floor, it can mess up the whole ecosystem! That's why we need to be careful and protect our oceanic friends!

Across

2. Can camouflage to get out of danger

5. Venom is more deadly than a cobra

7. Can regrow their spines and entire limbs

9. Largest animal to ever exist

10. Creature called polyps

11. These types of creatures find a mate and stay with them forever.

Down

1. They're known to travel in a group called pods

3. Temperature can determine the gender of these animals before hatching.

4. Shark that has eyes located on the sides of their flat head.

6. Can jump out of the water almost looking like a pizza coming out of the oven.

8. They're over 700 million years old.

12. Mistaken for whales but they're actually dolphins

Mini Game! Lets see how much you learned

A big thank you!

So we've wrapped up Trent's Adventures: Deep Sea Discovery, and it's been a blast having you along for the ride! From exploring coral to hanging out with octopuses and dolphins,we've seen it all.

Big thanks for being part of the gang! Trent and I had a ton of fun, and guess what? More adventures are headed your way. Get ready for more surprises, laughs, and a splash of excitement in the next round. Keep being curious and looking out for our fantastic ocean!

Author's Note:

I'm a scuba instructor, and in "Trent's Adventures: Deep Sea Discovery,"
I'm sharing some cool stuff straight from my underwater experiences.
It's not just from books; I wanted to make sure you get a taste of the ocean,
like you're right there with me.

*Smithsonian Ocean. "Smithsonian Ocean." Smithsonian Ocean.
https://ocean.si.edu/.*

*MarineBio Conservation Society. "MarineBio Conservation Society
." MarineBio Conservation Society. https://www.marinebio.org/.*

*Parker, Dianna. "Garbage Patches." OR&R's Marine Debris Program, 1
1 July 2013. https://marinedebris.noaa.gov/info/patch.html.*

Made in the USA
Las Vegas, NV
21 February 2024

86024211R00017